Going Viral

T0364576

Written by James Catchpole

Illustrated by Jennifer Latham Robinson

Collins

Chapter 1

Jack had been practising football in the garden all week, but it wasn't really big enough, what with all of Mum's flowers – the ones that were still standing.

So Dad said: "Why don't we try the park?" And Mum said that was an *excellent* idea.

Jack wasn't so sure. He was used to people staring
at him, but they stared even more when he kicked
a football at the park.

There probably won't be many *kids with one leg kicking*
footballs, he thought.

And he was right about that. But it was OK.

When they got to the park, Jack and Dad practised their passing-and-moving. People were stopping to watch, but it didn't feel like they were staring. At least, not in a bad way. They didn't look worried or sad (Jack's worst kind of stare). They looked happy.

As usual, after a few minutes of passing-and-moving,
Dad had to sit down for a bit, so Jack practised his
keepy-uppys.

One boy looked like he might be taking a video on
his phone, which felt a bit odd, but Dad gave the boy
a hard stare and he wandered off.

Some kids of about Jack's age started up a game.
Jack counted five on one team, and four on the other.
The kids were shouting and laughing. It looked fun.

It would be even more fun, Jack thought, *if I could join
the team with four players.*

They were all right at football, these kids. They weren't *too* good, so Jack knew he could keep up with them, if they let him play. But they hadn't seen him passing the ball with Dad. And no one ever believed he could play, unless they'd seen him.

Chapter 2

Jack was about to kick the ball at Dad to see if he'd get up again, when an older kid came over with a phone in his hand.

"Can you do any tricks?" he asked. And while Jack was trying to think how to reply, the kid added, "Give it here, I'll show you."

And he started juggling the ball. He caught it suddenly
between his heels, just above the ground, and then,
looking back over his shoulder, he rolled the ball from
one heel to the other and flipped it up, over his head.

Jack knew that trick. He'd seen it on Kick Tock. It was
a rainbow flick, and as it happened, he *had* worked
out how to do it – well, his own version, anyway.

So when the kid passed the ball back to him, Jack
stepped towards it, tapped the top of it with his crutch
and flipped it, as it bounced, with his heel. It flew up
over his head, and as it came down to the ground,
Jack trapped it under his boot.

"Oh. My. Days," said the kid. He looked like he'd just won a prize. "I've got to get this!" He was already swiping at his phone. "Please let me get this – "

Jack glanced at Dad, but he was busy on his own phone.

"Just do that again," said the kid. "Trust me, this could be *massive*."

The truth was, Jack *was* proud of that trick. It was his best trick. Though he hadn't expected it to have quite that effect.

Well, why not? thought Jack.

"OK," he said.

When the kid was ready with his phone, Jack did the trick again. And this time, he did it even better.

"Got it!" said the kid.

"Got what?" asked Dad.

"It's a video," said the kid, speaking fast.
"It's for Kick Tock. I'm on Kick Tock. I do
football skills. I'm deejayonionbag. Have you
seen my stuff? No? Oh. Really? I've got
a thousand subscribers! It doesn't matter.
This matters – look – "

And he showed Dad the video he'd just taken.
"This is another level. This is going to go *so* viral.
Please say I can post it?"

Jack was sure Dad would say no, but he asked to see the video again. Maybe he was proud of Jack's trick, too. Because then he said: "What do you reckon, Jack? You don't have to say yes, just because deejayparsnips wants you to."

The kid didn't look very happy, but he kept quiet and looked down at his shoes. Jack noticed he had his fingers crossed.

"Do you want a thousand people to see your trick?" asked Dad. "Or shall we tell deejaybroccoli thanks, but no thanks?"

Jack tried to think about it.
Was a thousand people seeing him
the same as a thousand people staring
at him? Maybe letting the kid post it
was a bad idea.

Then again, a thousand people
seeing him play football meant
a thousand people believing he
could play football. And that had
to be good, hadn't it? Hadn't it?!

"OK," he said.

Immediately, the kid started tapping on his phone, faster and faster, like he thought Jack might change his mind at any moment. Then one last tap and he looked up, grinning. "Done!" he said. "Cheers!"

And off he went, staring at his phone like it might know a trick of its own.

"Sandwich?" asked Dad.

It was lunchtime, after all. And Jack was definitely hungry. The parents of the kids from the big game seemed to have had the same idea. Everyone was taking a break.

Jack was about to tuck in when Dad's phone started buzzing.

"Mum says Uncle Charlie's been calling," he muttered. "What's he so excited about?"

Then there was a little silence, which made Jack look up. "What is it?"

"It's the video," said Dad, still staring at his phone. "It's deejaywhat'shisface – "

"Have a thousand people seen it?" Jack was starting to feel excited now.

"It's actually … a few more than that." And he passed Jack his phone.

Chapter 3

There was Jack, in the park, doing his trick. Underneath was a little round picture of the kid, grinning, and some words he must have written:

ONE-LEGGED KID BREAKS
INTERNET WITH
FOOTBALL TRICK!

Jack knew he *was* a "one-legged kid", but it wasn't what he called himself. So that felt a bit odd. But Dad was pointing to where it said "views". There was a number – 473.

Jack felt a little disappointed, which he knew was silly because that was easily more than all the kids in his school.

"Do you know what the 'K' stands for?" asked Dad. "K means a thousand. That's 473,000. Oops – not any more – "

The number had flicked over to 500K, while they were watching.

"Oh," said Jack. "Oh, wow! Isn't that, like, half a *million*?"

"Yes, that's half a million views," said Dad.

"And look," said Dad. "There are already over *2,000* comments – "

And there really were. In several different languages.

"Amazing!"

"Herrlich!!!"

"Incroyable!!"

The funny thing was, when Dad asked his phone to translate them, it turned out they all said the same four or five things, over and over again.

"So INSPIRING!"

"He's better than me with two legs!"

"That's one brave kid."

"NEVER GIVE UP!"

And every so often, someone would say, "Aww – so sad," which Jack tried his best to ignore.

"Why do grown-ups all say the same stuff?"

"That's a good question," said Dad.

Chapter 4

When he'd seen enough, Jack asked Dad if they could go home again. He wanted to tell Mum about what had happened, and maybe not see anyone he didn't know for the rest of the day.

Jack wasn't sure how he felt about the video. It was mind-boggling that so many people all around the world had seen his trick, and some of their family and friends had messaged Dad to say, "Well done!" But the words and comments on the video sounded like they were talking about someone else – someone who wasn't real.

He was thinking about it all as they passed the football game.

"Emily! Be careful!" said a grown-up, as the ball rolled over to Jack. "Sorry!" she said, to Dad.

Jack knew what this meant. It meant she was worried he might have been hurt. By the ball, the gently rolling ball. Because no one *ever* believed he could actually *play* football.

That was it. There was only one thing for it. Jack gave her a hard stare and kicked the ball back to the other kids, as hard as he could.

"I ... yeah ... I wouldn't worry – " said Dad.

"Oh," said the girl, who must have been Emily.
"Can you play football?"

"Obviously," said Jack, who had decided not to care
what anyone thought, for the rest of the day.

Not that Emily seemed to notice. Because then she
said, "Do you want to play? We need one more – "

And Jack realised he did. He *really* did.

"What do you reckon, Jack?" asked Dad, smiling.

Jack smiled too.

"OK," he said.

Jack's journey

excited

wondering

inquisitive

proud

30

uncertain

confused

thoughtful

happy

31

Ideas for reading

Written by Christine Whitney
Primary Literacy Consultant

Reading objectives:
- make inferences on the basis of what is being said and done
- answer and ask questions
- predict what might happen on the basis of what has been read so far
- discuss and clarify the meanings of words
- discuss the sequence of events in books and how items of information are related

Spoken language objectives:
- participate in discussions
- use spoken language to develop understanding through speculating, hypothesising, imagining and exploring ideas
- ask relevant questions

Curriculum links: Computing: recognise common uses of information technology beyond school; use technology safely and respectfully, keeping personal information private; identify where to go for help and support when they have concerns about content or contact on the internet or other online technologies

Interest words: viral, mind-boggling, subscribers

Word count: 1482

Build a context for reading

- Look at the title on the front cover, then the illustration. Encourage children to share their understanding of what the book will be about. Check understanding of the word *viral*.
- Read the blurb on the back cover. Ask children to suggest what might happen to Jack. Do they have any advice for him?
- Without singling out, encourage children who are comfortable doing so to share their experiences of disability.

Understand and apply reading strategies

- Read Chapter 1 together. Ask children to explain what the reader now knows about Jack, his mum and his dad.
- Continue to read together up to the end of Chapter 2. Ask children to summarise the advice that Dad gives to Jack about the video.